Teenager by Oluwaseun

Teenager by Oluwaseun

Bamgbopa Oluwaseun Sunday

Copyright © 2011 by Bamgbopa Oluwaseun Sunday.

ISBN: Softcover   978-1-4653-6618-4
          Ebook   978-1-4653-6619-1

All rights reserved. No part of this book may be reproduced or transmitted in any form or by any means, electronic or mechanical, including photocopying, recording, or by any information storage and retrieval system, without permission in writing from the copyright owner.

This book was printed in the United States of America.

To order additional copies of this book, contact:
Xlibris Corporation
0-800-644-6988
www.xlibrispublishing.co.uk
Orders@xlibrispublishing.co.uk
302816

Contents

ACKNOWLEDGEMENT 9
PREFACE 11
INTRODUCTION 13
EARLY TEEN 15
GROWING UP 19
LOVE 27
FRIENDS 31
FREEDOM 35
CHALLENGES 37
CONCLUSION 43
NOTES 45

I dedicate this book to all the teenagers out there.
I was once in your shoes.

You with the sad eyes don't be discouraged; I realize it's hard to take courage in the world full of people, You can lose sight of it all and darkness still inside you make you feels so small. But I see your true colours shining through, so don't be afraid to let them show.

Life is a teacher, but it doesn't give you the answer, it only point out the ways and let you make your own choices, your own mistakes. That way you will learn and then you get all the glory and you will ultimately and eventually deserve it.

ACKNOWLEDGEMENT

To God be the glory; this book was made possible by my most loving and caring parents. I acknowledge them for their tremendous moral and financial supports towards the successful completion of this book.

Their contributions toward the successful completion of this book were so numerous and invaluable that this space will be grossly inadequate to fully express all.

I am also indebted to xlibris publishing company Dartford UK for the publishing and printing of my first book. I am looking forward to work with them more often.

PREFACE

My motivation towards this book was from the saying that goes thus "time is an asset, you never get it back". The idea behind this book occur to me one night when I was meditating and thinking about my life and what I went through during the day. I always do that every night but I discovered that the next day even hold a new and interesting experience for me and on a wider range, my experience daily is so much similar literally to my fellow teenager. And to be candid this boils down to the facts that at that delicate age of ours, we all so much have similar needs, are in nearly the same position and we all think, react or behave similarly.

But for the reasons that we are different as human being gives rises to our different ways of life literally, we all have the same goal. What is in the thought of many teens is to grow up, go to a standard and recognise school both high school and some might even want to go to college and after that, to get a good job in a reputable company and have kids and then live their life to the fullest.

As I was meditating on these, I discovered that there are other generations of teens coming after us and they will definitely be in our shoes someday, and probably they might require some possible words of encouragement and experience for their present situation and am afraid they might found none.

In view of this, I put it upon myself to put some of my teenage experiences into a book so as to serve the benefits of some teenagers that are coming behind and to tell them what life and time holds for them all . . .

INTRODUCTION

Congratulations on your new born baby. At least your prayers had been answered. God has done his own part by granting you your wishes of a bouncing baby, now is the time for you to do your own part. The baby growing up is now completely left to you; bring him up in a way that he will be useful to you, himself and the entire world at large.

This is my story I would say I was born with a silver spoon because my parent never lack anything they wished for, they were blessed and I also came to them as blessing as well. Did you know the joy that came along side with my birth, guess so . . . at least the way I was told, I was welcomed to this planet on the 21th of may and christened on the eight day like every other kids. I happen to be the first son of my father who turn out to be in his early twenties. He was so much young as at that time but he still gather enough resources to support my growth. I was brought up like every other kid. I started school at a very early age which am proud of and was told that I was cool, brilliant and stubborn as at that time. I guess they were right because I don't really know myself back then and I can't really argue with whatever behaviours or features they said I had back then but from what I was told, I really had the cause to judge myself as being totally stubborn with respect to the scenario I performed of breaking one of my classmate bone in the cause of a bed fight which was supported by most of my friends back then in boarding school . . . .

During my course of growing up, I discovered a lot of things about life. I learnt how growing up could be and how it could affect a lot of people. I learnt about different people, their ways, behaviours, languages, foods, locations etc and how all these things could affect their mentality and their level of reasoning. I learnt that we all see the world in a different perspective and all have different opinion about what is and what might have been.

I learnt how parent could be of influence in the growing up and development of their wards. I hope you will agree with me that growth and development are not the same thing. In my own words, I will say growth is the increase in size of something while development is an advanced growth whereby the child will not only increase in size but also increase in knowledge and wisdom and have the ability to think rationally and do things that commands wonder. The ability to see the world in a different ways and the ability to think of how to make a mark. All of these I call development and they can only be achieved if the foundation of the child is solid and had not been jeopardized.

EARLY TEEN

My early teen was so great for me; it was full of fun and enjoyable moment. It was full of pleasing and satisfying occasions. It was also filled with disturbing and distressing experiences. But most of all I learnt my lessons and I carry my experiences everywhere I go. It was in my early teens that I started discovering things that eventually showed me what reality really was. Day by day I learnt new and challenging things. Everything became clearer and clearer to me. I will say I was just getting started to meet with reality. To know what is like to feel something and be able to explain why and how those things came to me and not somebody else.

Some things happened to me that I can't really explain not because I was dumb but because my brain was not equipped enough yet to comprehend those explanations or better still because I haven't gotten enough experience to enhance those conditions. But as I grew up, I got more clarity to my situation and my world and immediate environment experience these sudden and rapid changes.

I was in my middle teens when my father had the cause to travel to the UK to search for greener pastures. He thought in his mind that by the next few years, he might not have the ability or resources to cater for us again. That is what I like about him, he always project and plan ahead for the future needs and he would not just stop at that but also put up strategy to make these work. With the help of his beloved wife they started planning towards this goal just to make it a reality. They both tried hard and met lots of challenging situations and obstacles on the way. Achieving this goal seems so tough when he went to the embassy twice and was not awarded his visa due to some shortcomings that was created. He went through lots and with the total support of his faithful wife; their latter surpass their former, I mean their effort was granted with success.

My father finally left on the 18th of august 2004, this day was a very important day in our lives, as for me, I won't says I should be glad or sad because at that delicate age of mine, I have reasons to do both. To be happy in the sense that one of my family member is going abroad and you all know what that means, it means sooner or later, I have hope of being a universal citizen through that inevitable advantage. I also have reasons to be sad and that is because am going to miss him so much. I believe that at that delicate age of mine, I need my dad more than anybody else, to do some stuff together, to teach me things as regards my current age, to talk to him on several issues and hoping to find clarity in his words and also his advice for me as a teen because he had once been in my shoes. There are some impacts that he has to make in my life that is still missing till today. But all the same I was happy for him as his dream came true that fateful day. As a family, we all prayed together and bid him farewell in his endeavour.

After he was gone, he called the third day that he had arrived safely in London and that everything was alright. It was then that I realized that he will miss some of my years as a teenager. I was also stuck with my mum to take care of me and my siblings' but I won't emphasis on this but to be candid, she really did a good job in bringing us all up and she took part in most if not all of my teenage years. We were all brought up in the best way I could ever think off and we all have the fear of God at heart. If you are wondering about the word 'we', am referring to me and my three siblings' two girls and a boy.

During my early teens, I started my high school experience which was at first awkward because I have never been in amidst of large number of people before for the reason that we have more pupils in class compare to my former school and this was kind of freaking me out. Nevertheless I started to blend in and adjusting to my new life which I later found interesting thereafter. High school was educative for me, I met lots of friends and I am proud to say that they were friends for life because we all still get in touch up till date and they are all doing fine same as I am.

GROWING UP

Growing up, I will say is not easy and a hell lots of tasks because it involves lots of challenging things. It involves you trying to adapt and endure with your everyday activities. All this boils down to the very first day of our lives, I mean individual life. The very first sound you hear, your very first sight, and the very first perception of your other senses to life. Their perception at first and their eagerness and ability to scale through, all these really matter and a whole lot of people reacts to these differently.

After our own reactions and feeling about life and nature comes our first teacher I tagged parent. They are our very first guardian and teacher. Most kids spend most of their time with their parent, these times means something to their life, it is either full of learning and lot of developmental strategy or it is just a kind of formal introduction or identity between the parents and their wards. Their entry into our life is a very delicate and precious one. Their presence is a needed one but might take the wrong turn if proper care is not taking. At a tender age, they are the closest to us and any image they portray will easily be adapted by us because at our early stage of life, our brain is very much ready to learn and attract even to every bit of information or display. As we grew up, parents tend to make decisions for us, they are right in doing that for us but for it to be perfect it has to be in our own best interest. These I believe many parents want and are willing to do even if there are obstacles on the way but in some cases some might overdo these and it end up taken the wrong turns and unpleasant results.

During my cause of growing up, I tend to learn every day, everything became clearer and better to me. Everything I thought is mystery keep unveiling itself every day. My parents were both there for me; they brought me up in a very nice and humble way. I have them to thanks for this. From the time I was old enough and my senses were clear to me, I have been trained to adapt to every condition I found myself. I was brought up to appreciate nature and all it inhabitants, I was taught how to react and behave to every situation that comes my way. All these I wasn't taught directly but indirectly. I tend to draw lessons from every scenario that presents its self. I learn to let go when it worth it and also to always take risk when I actually known it worth it as well. The most interesting thing I learn is to appreciate nature and be conscious of our environment. I lack some aspect of this training because I didn't appreciate my environment well enough and it really affected me because I lost some vital informations that I could have used to my own advantage in amidst my peers for example, I am not that good in polities, a bit behind in sports and maybe some other discussion topics among my friends of the same peers. I believe in one thing and it is really clear to me and it is that you will not appreciate some things well enough until you lose or need them badly and they are out of reach or out of sight. So since then, I learnt to take things or every pieces of information at my disposal as serious and precious as possible.

I also learnt that locality also matters in our growing up stage. Let consider a child that lives in a well structured apartment in a suitable environment and a child that lives otherwise. I notice that during their cause of growing up, their mentality, mode of learning, brain capacity differs provided all other factors being equal. This is nature at work. I can't really explain this fact but you will agree with me that it is because both kids have different friends, environment, exposure, needs, and attitude and so on.

With all these facts, I can proudly say that our brain develops according to how we challenged it; I mean our exposure, the songs we listen to, the books we read, the friends we keep, and the level of information at our disposal, our day to day activities and so on. You will agree with me if I say that **information is life**. Where we are presently is a factor of the various information at our disposal. A man without information is a corpse yet living. With these, I will establish the fact that every teen have different sense of reasoning that is we all approach an issue in different direction and perspective. I also admit the fact that we all learn every day, and there is no age limit to learning, anybody can be a source of valuable information at any time of the day and paying attention to those informations is another critical stage we have to undergo.

During my cause of growing I also learnt that we make decisions every day, either tough or easy ones, but either ways, it still make or marks an absolute change and turn around in our lives. Many teens are not aware of the fact that they are responsible for the consequence or corollary that comes out of their decision whether now or later. Some teen are really hard to predicts, they tends to do something that command wonders sometimes, every teen want to wake up one day and find everything in order, in fact not even the way they recently left it. Some teen don't fancy taking responsibility and learning from them. We all want to sit down and watch someone else get it done for us.

I believe everyone or probably every teen is a leader but it now rest on individual shoulder to accept it or not. Being a leader is a critical decision and being able to challenge your world view, being able to forgo individual pleasure for the benefits of other individuals and be rest assured to have no regrets thereafter. A leader is not a title which individual occupies but rather it is in everyone to take advantage of in changing the world. At least that was the purpose of our existence, to change the world and make it a better place for every individual to inhabit. Flexible thinking and determination is the key, knowledge and wisdom is another.

I will make an illustration in the field of science, technology and arts, since 18's through the early 19's century to this present moment, lots of inventions and creativity had been made possible, lots of equipments had been developed and design for the benefits of the world at large. All these started from hypothesis and a critical view of the earth in need of something. The creation of problems that had not yet occurs is of note, followed by an intensive research and success thereafter. It occurs to me that these people sense some things that ought to have been and they worked years to make it a reality. I thought to myself that over these years of intensive research and invention, that all had been discovered I mean there is nothing left to be discovered. But my instinct tells me that I was very much wrong. This planet is a dynamics one, Therefore there are lots of things and inventions that are seriously waiting for we teens to unveil them for the benefits of our own generation. We have to think rationally and make it done. If the earliest people can do justice to these things then we can as well if we all are ready to prioritize it and work together as one.

Everybody is different in one way or the other, I personally always feel different, but as a matter of facts, the real difference in me is yet to be demonstrated and I will say that am working on it, very soon my work will announce my presence. This should also be in the mind of all teens to make sure that they make a mark so that they will always be remembered for good. Some people tend to do comparism, I mean comparing one person to the other. Trying to look out for what is good in first people and using it against the other. This is really absurd because it make one person feel inferior to the other. I also feel inferior sometime when I notice that some or one of my mate is unto something that is of note, something that pronounce his presence and people around are praising him for a job well done, I feel inferior and that is always like a motivation to me in the sense that I make sure that I also announce my presence through something of note too. If these are the nature of most teen and youth of today, I mean competing with inventions, theories and explanations of some phenomenon which they came in contact with as a result of the thirst and hunger for knowledge through some weird motivation, then the world would be better. Likewise some people are ready and will do everything in their power to manipulate you to their own advantage. When people are inferior to you as a result of your brilliant work, they tend to manipulate you to be like them and if you are not that lucky you end up losing the sight of success. I believe firstly that everybody feels for him or herself before even thinking about others, therefore the issue and power of comparism should not be over emphasised.

During my cause of growing up, I learnt the meaning of the word birthday and why most people celebrate it. Some people just celebrate it but clearly they have no idea what it was. They have a unique date once in a year to enjoy themselves probably with friends. My own conception about the word birthday is that it is a day that an individual was born, a day we all step into this very world. Our first breath started that day and we all made our first sound of joy which sounded exactly like the opposite but is precisely a cry of joy. That very faithful day, we brought joy and happiness to many people and many homes. Our presence was a blessing and some other people are in expectance of such a bountiful joy. The whole world rejoices on our arrival.

Starting from that day, we all grew older and older every day, right from the first minute, we began to adapt to our new and permanent environment (earth). We were initially taken care of until when we can look out for ourselves. Right from the time we knew our left from our right, we began to learn the ways and manners to behave and react in environment we found ourselves. But I will establish the fact that we all learn every day but the friends, schools, environment etc in which we found ourselves is a function of who we are and what we will stand for in the nearby future. Therefore every individual was born the same way but have different vision and mission based on their respective orientation right from birth up till present.

There is a saying that age is just a number but the lives in our life are what really count. I will say this is true, I got the motivation on one of my friend's birthday party. He always celebrates his birthday every year, always rejoicing for another added year and giving thanks to God. What motivated me that day was that on one of his birthday card, there was an inscription which says **"how many lives have you impacted, are you living or just existing"**. This message really touched me so much that I wondered what a motivational message. With my own point of view I believe celebrating birthday every year is as good as celebrating each year close to death which am very much right about, but it is also celebrating our achievements and victory over the last few years and also the lives in our life. Therefore I will say each time we celebrate our birthday, we should have something specific to celebrate and be joyous about and by so doing it will help us work hard and prepare for the next birthday which will also be much more cheerful and joyful than the previous ones and it goes on and on.

Remember we all live for somebody else and that person is expecting so much from us. Let us set the pace and leave our mark on the sand of time and not just pass without any notice. So that when we are finally gone the whole world will wept on our departure but will forever celebrate our Names.

So far, I have learnt to seek and know the reason behind every mystery. With these on my mind, the question "why?" always came to mind. This question gives rises to other questions like how, where, what, when? And so on. It is a very good reason to know why we want to embark on something, it really gives us the insight of what is being required of us and the obstacles we are likely to meet on the way. **Why** is a question for our existence, our behaviours, activities, intensions etc. if this question is not properly attended to, then other question that comes after it are in serious state of dilemma. If we know the reason behind the things we do or tend to do, then we'll be able to contemplate maybe our reason are good enough and are in the best interest of not only ourselves but other individuals at large. After the **why** question had been answered, then other questions following it will all be answered at ease and at the end of the day, success will be achieved. I will quote from Oluwaseun in 2010 that **"why is why we live"**.

I have also learnt so far that our character and the way we behave really matters a lot. They say attitude determine altitude. That is very much true because individual potentials will always catapult him/her to greater height but our character will determine how far. Therefore our character matter most to everybody around us, the way we treat people, the respect we accord them and so on. I will say everybody is very much important literally and I have learnt that we all need one another to survive and no matter what, we'll always need one another. This boils down to the fact that some individuals are not treated the way they wanted to be treated and they end up compromising themselves to suit the needs and favour of others. We should be proud of who we are and to stand by it any time of the day even to the end of the world. I don't think anyone decision will make my life unless I am kind of inferior to them. I always say to myself that if people don't like me for who I am, that is their problem because they have so many things they will lose and not the other way round, therefore I will not compromise myself to meet their needs rather I'll just be myself. I want to be known for what I am and what I can be.

Growing up, we all make mistake either due to bad decisions or other reasons and the consequences of those mistakes still haunt us up till date. Anytime I looked back and wondered what might have been, I always wish I could go back in time and make things right, but these I know that it is impossible to go back in time to correct my wrong doings so I have to move on and make sure I committed fewer or even no mistakes again. It always sucks to learn from one's mistake but I think it make me have a unique experience regarding that aspect and I will be qualified enough to give other people advice with respect to that because I have been there and know what it takes and how it feels to be there. I won't say am proud of that because learning from own mistake is always not good because for a lesson well learnt, you would have suffered some notable loss and that is what makes it an unforgettable and remarkable experience. In the other way round it is different from wisdom which is learning from other peoples' mistakes so as to prevent they themselves from making the same. That I will say is the difference between wisdom and knowledge because knowledge is affiliated with experience. That is my own definition though.

LOVE

Love is a crucial issue that every teens face. It is a game of power and manipulation of emotions, especially the late teens. They tend to misinterprets it for something else. They often try to define it to suit their own personal purpose, they even pretend they know all about it, but eventually they all turns out to have no idea about love.

Love is best described than defined, many people tried to define it in their own respective ways but it all boils down to just one singular fact, and that is to have great affection for someone or something unconditionally, I mean without any string attached. Love I will say is very mysterious. It really works perfectly for some and turns out bad for others but either way, we get to learn our lessons. Love is a delicate thing and should be handled with outmost care or it might turn out to be a thing of regrets. Love should not be based on fantasy; I mean like a castle in the air which has no solid foundation. You will agree with me that it is bound to fall anytime but I have learnt so far that love is always certain no matter what; the feelings and emotions will always still be there.

As a teen we all want to have this mysterious feeling as early as possible, in my own case I have so much long to feel it and to know what it encompass. I want to know every detail of it not just be learning or reading about it, but also by experimenting it. This urgent need was just simply as a result of wisdom from other people actions and the thought of not been equal with them. This gives me worries because it sadden my mind to not feel or experience what my other mates are experiencing, it like am lacking behind and I really want to fasten my seat belt and find a solution to this lateness. So at first I summon some courage to date some few girls but in most cases, it happen that I am not yet ready or inexperienced to play this new and interesting game and that I need to be a little more patient and relax to be able to feel and understand the scope. Later on to my biggest surprise, I had this feeling at first I don't know what it was but I just keep feeling this bond, joy and eagerness to see this person and before I knew it I just can't help it anymore. It is then that I knew and realized that I was in love.

This is my story, I will say love to me was a very beautiful thing; it is really real and genuine. I met this girl in my first year in college, I was so much attracted to her and I think she was attracted to me as well. It was really hard to pass my message across, I mean my desires and intension to be her friend, she happens to be my first love because I had a unique feelings when I met her and this fact really blinded me because I hope in my mind that I have finally found my missing rib. As a guy, I work out my strategy on how to approach my flower and to pour out my heart burden. This girl on the other side is expecting my invitation. She knew I was coming due to the facts that I had displayed to her some awareness of my intensions like some interesting, lovely and romantic text messages, a cute smile whenever we are in class waiting for lectures and some other essential means. I let the cat out of the bag one faithful day by telling her how I felt about her and also that I was into her I mean I had a crush on her and am so serious about it. I was glad I did spill my mind open to her and later I was chilling for my response which I wasn't expecting through words but actions. These actions never came, I waited long enough before I started portraying my own action then I notice something, this girl is really ready to be friends with me, I mean she was also into me for real but she is not yet satisfied with her experience as regards relationship. She wants to have stories to share and it is as if the right man came too early and she wasn't expecting that early. She wanted to act like someone that is an expert in teenage relationship welfare but she is inexperienced yet, she perspire to have a number of relationships as possible to be experienced, therefore she wanted to acquire that skill. I sense that she wanted me but not that early yet, so she wanted to keep me close long enough till she gets what she wanted. That was a loss on my side because I will have to adapt and endure to every situation that I found myself in.

That I will say is unfair because common interests are the key to romance but since we both lack it, love had to wept on our behave. For a perfect love life, each partner has to accept each other the way they are and then brand them the way they want them to be. Love is not about finding the perfect person, but making the imperfect person perfect.

Many teens have different perspective about love, some people tend to play hard to get game, and this is just to study the other person behaviour, endurance, adaptability and so on and also to find out if the person's feeling is real. But I will say this method is not right. There is a saying that says get what you want at the right and quality time. This quality time will now enhance the compatibility flow and at the end of the day, both partners will get each other right. I do believe in love at first sight I mean meeting someone today and falling for the person naturally and vice versa. This is very great but if this affair is not properly manages, it might led to crashing because there is tendency for each partner at his own convenience to portray or display some sets of new behaviours that might be of adverse or unfavourable effect to the other partner. I will say when meeting a new person and there is a boiling intension to be friend with, the best thing to do is to act normal, I mean being oneself. There is this urge to do everything to please the other person, trying to portray some character you are not capable of, trying to Bragg so as to impress the other partner. These acts are not usually nice because it make you feel inferior to the other person, it just like you are trying to achieve something from the person approval of you. There is a believe of mine and a favourite quote as well by Oluwaseun that says "**you**

don't find love but rather love finds you". I also believed that we don't choose who to love; it just happened, therefore when love does find you, all your senses must be working together towards being your normal self and not your new self due to the strange appearance of some new being.

Trying to get somebody badly is another issue I have to emphasis on, because it seldom occur that we have to a lot of teens out there where by one partner tends to want to get the other at all cost irrespective of anything that might happen thereafter. Though I will say love is very strong and it require a high level of affinity for each other but if that affinity is not properly control and manage, it can lead to the loss of dignity and values and also loss of worth. These I agree are very sad because the best thing is now turning the other way round and it will not be in the best interest of the individual in question. When talking about dignity, it is a serious quality of being worthy of self respect and also self importance. These I say everybody have but most of us tend to lose it easily at the expense of something arbitrary or imaginary. Anything we do, we should have at the back of our mind that our works and values will always speak for us even far above what we even imagined or expected. Therefore trying to show case all these features will only make them fade or goes into extinction. Love is real and love is you.

FRIENDS

It is inevitable for an average teen to have friends at least one or two. You will all agree with me that friends are not avoidable, at least at that tender age of growth. Friends I will say are unavoidable acquaintances that we get to meet during our cause of growing up. They usually partake in almost all of our endeavours. In some cases they usually made decisions for us but they are not always responsible for the outcome of those decisions.

When I say friends, I mean important people and personalities around us; those that witness some case study in my life. If there is one thing I've learned in life, it is that friends are ultimately everything (aside from families) moreover, I even consider my Friends my Family. I regard everybody I know as my friend only that they get to fall in different category with respect to the level of importance. To start with, I classified my parent as my friends; at least both of them were my first and closest companion. They raise and trained me up to this present moment. I can boldly say I owe everything to them. They are the best, drum rolls to them please.

I have real friends and bad friends. When it comes to real friends they are usually my friends indeed. We all know the category we fall into. But as for me I will say that those that are close enough to be my good and real friends have good things to say about me. They know that they will never be in-need as long as I have; they know that I have their backs every time and am sure that they also have mine. They also know that I love life and I always try as much as possible to enjoy it to the fullest. I regard life as a gift from Mother Nature, It is a gift that has been given to us all and it should not be taken for granted nor should it be wasted rather it should be handled with uttermost care and tranquillity.

With my friends around me, I am always honest, stable, secure and tolerant; I try to choose my words wisely and I am sure that as a friend, I am one of the most loving people you will ever want to meet in case you have not met me before. What you see is definitely not all, there is much within that has not yet been unveiled, so come on board and together we will all enjoy nature.

During my tender age as a teen, I have a quite number of friends which had made or mark my life up till date. They all made a remarkable spot in my life, some I am proud of and others I don't want to talk about. I will say all these spot in my life are at my own very discretion because I permit their influence in my life. And with my experience about friends, I will say I can successfully describe most of my friends, I mean all what I know about them based on my acquaintances with them and how they have influence my being either for good or the opposite.

I have a friend that is very jovial with me, he takes everything that concerns me personal, he always want to be with me and be involves in my everyday doing but not literally. We both talk about stuff and I will say I am free and so much confident about him. His ways challenged me and I get to learn from him every day which he doesn't literally know about. We hang out together, do crazy stuffs together, gist about our future and what the world holds for us and our inevitable relevance to the globe at large. I am proud of him and I will say if more friends like him are on this planet, then the world will be the best and safest place to be.

I have another friend that is completely the opposite. Though I call him my friend because there are some little things we use to do together as friends like attends lectures, hang out after school closes and go to parties and other extra activities together. These various activities really made me to see and access the real him. I learnt so many things about him that I am not proud about and all my efforts to influence him positively prove fruitless. Some of his attribute is that he talks a lot, very lazy and unintelligent, slow and so on. I know that one of my duties as a friend to him is to be able to influence him with my positive side and to also gain in his own affirmative side as well but he was not just responding to merge. Instead he is influencing me totally with his disparaging side unknowing to both of us, but when I sense the change, I immediately took caution.

I have friends of various nature and kind of behavioural pattern, I have friends that get angry when you don't call them and I have those that don't care whether you do or not, I have friends that cover my back in my absence and I have those that intimidate me even in my presence. I have friends that always want me to be behind them and I have those that want us to move side by side. I have friends that envy me when I have good grade, I have those that make jest of me when I am the last in the class. I have friends that seek me out when am sick and I have those that sniff their nose and turn their back on me. I have friends that entrust valuable things to me for safety and I have those that accuse me of stealing their gold. I have friends that want the best for me and I have those that inquire me to bow before them. I have friends that love me for who I am no matter what and I have those that ask me to go to hell

With all these connection and a great level of acquaintance with these people, I hope you will agree with me that there is a great lesson being learn in having different categories of friends who also sees the world differently and that a great bond may have been established with some of them especially the best and closest of them all and that it will be hard to let go, especially with those that a great bond had been established with but to part ways with those that are not too close is not even an easy thing to do as well since we have already shared some memorable moments together.

I will say it is so easy to make friends but difficult to dissolve. I had this experience in my college days when I was in a position to render help to one of my class mate in terms of accommodation.

Initially, the person in question was my friend but the friendship bond was not that serious, I will say it was still in low state of value. But believe me or not after I started living with this friend, we both talked together all the time, sleep read and do most things together, I admit my world changed drastically. Lots of things change about me that I owe to him but by the time he was leaving, I knew I had made a bond with him and am going to miss him badly for what we had shared.

Life comes with no Guarantees but with real and good friends, there is hope. Life offers no time out but with friends, there are lots of things to look forward to. Life offers no second chances but with cool friend there is also hope. Love life to the fullest, but be constantly conscious of the friends you keep because friends will affect your life either positively or the opposite.

Laugh as much as you can, Spend all your money in the world, Tell someone what they meant to you, Speak out your mind even in public, Dance in the pouring rain, fall asleep watching the sun come up, Stay up late, Be a flirt, Smile until your face hurts, Don't be afraid to take chances or fall in love, Hold someone in the hand, Comfort a friend, be involved in lot of things and most of all live in the moment and enjoy most of your time with people you love because when you look back someday with your Grey hair and you have no regrets, It's going to be what will makes you smile.

Friends are indeed our companion but their intervention in our endeavours should have a limit.

FREEDOM

Freedom is a beautiful thing every teen will ever imagine, the situation or act whereby the teen has to do almost everything on his/her own. This stage is very crucial and to my own point of view, I will say it had to come at the late teen or probably early twenties because there are some skills which the teen need to have acquired to be able to survive this stage. This stage is a life time stage; it is a continuous process whereby decision making will be decided by the individual himself.

Life is a series of choices and a big combination of moment; little moments add up to big ones and create who we are. Therefore this stage is important because it deals with a whole lot of things that pattern who we are and who we would later be. Things like academics, choice of friends, families, love and so on. The teen has to merge all these aspects together and be completely fine without any cause for alarm. This is very hard; I mean to combine all these things together without any mistake being made. Sure there will be mistake being made but how the teen learn from the mistake and move forward is a sign of maturity that the teen is completely able to handle any situation that present itself later on in future. Freedom is when you are in the position to make decision on your own and be ready to bear the consequences to the decision being made. It is the liberty you have to make choices and be of free-will where there is lack of restrictions on any choice being made and you had to enjoy your independence on your own. This is where you have to decide who you really want to be, is it the ambitious type, or the self centre and careless type. This stage will judge you. First of all, you have to admit that you now have responsibilities, I didn't mean you have to cater for yourself in term of finances and other parental responsibilities but what am trying to pass across is that you now have complete control of your well being, I mean your present and your future. You have to lay down your goals and narrow your day to day activities toward those goals so as to achieve them at your speculated time range. When these had become your activities in your freedom stage, then I will say you are set to face any challenge that comes your way thereafter. Because these stage is so full of challenges and the level of your choice making will help you scale through.

Pride is also a factor that presents itself at this stage. It is a sense of being independent and a sense of superior control over others. It is also a sense of dignity and self respect. These I say are very good to feel and are therefore inevitable for everyone especially teenagers. Many teen therefore took advantage of this factor to show their true self. They want to be superior and have total control of everything around them. They don't want to be left out in anything. For my response, I will say everybody has pride but mismanage of it leads to destruction.

CHALLENGES

Challenges are a very critical situation and as far as I am concerned it is so much confidential as well. For the last few years of my life, I have learnt who I am due to the challenges I came across, the ones I overcome and the ones which overcame me. I have learnt my strength and weakness, my opportunities and my threat. These make me who I am and probably what I am liable to become. I have experienced so many cases of challenges like the physical, emotional, educational, social challenges, but I am proud to say that I have scale through at least for now because I definitely know that more are on their ways and am not scared to welcome them all since I will learn from them all.

When I say physical challenges, you might not relate it to anything challenging at all but I know for sure that it is a challenge. They are the challenges that are so much obvious to us, I mean they are very real and it tends to need urgent and quick attention. I mean a challenge in the sense that trying to keep oneself in good shape and good state of health so as to be easily recognisable with one's fellow peers group or mate. It will really look awkward if in amidst your peers you obviously look or appear different due to the way you look or seem to be. These might be as a result of the different foods they all eat, exercises and the various physical materials they are all expose to. These in my own words I call physical challenge and many teens often go wrong in trying as much as possible to fit in so as to overcome this challenge and they go out of their ways to do nasty thing just to compromise themselves with. I understand the fact that we all in amidst of our peers wanted to be treated equally or the same way but if the resources to stay equal is limited, we end up compromising ourselves just to suit or fulfil that need in which we desire. These compromising issue should not be encourage anymore because it will always led to bad experiences.

Educational challenges are also very important and crucial in every teen's lives. This is even more challenging than I thought because an average teen has to be up and doing in his/her academics and the ability to compete with several teens and still be noticeable is a challenge on its own and the teen in question has to do everything in his/her capacity to be a able to stand out in amidst his/her peers.

For me education has not really been a challenge because of what it simply involves as regards my own point of view. I always attend classes and seldom read but I think when I do read, I always understand what I read and to combine with the previous knowledge in the class, I always come out in flying colours in my examination. But here is the challenging aspect, when I notice that some of my peers or class mate had more ideas in a particular subject than I do, I tend to push myself too hard so as to meet up with them before it get out of hand, I mean before the examination. During that period, am not always happy with myself and I blamed myself for that laziness and lackness behind. I term these challenges because as a teen, I have to be up to date as my mates are and not far behind them. But right now I will advise every teen not to compare themselves with anybody rather they should compare themselves with the standard.

There is a particular scenario I will love to share as regards education challenges. It happen to me and I always wondered, why will someone give or commits so much efforts and strength in something and at the end of it all get little or minimal from it. How do you think it will feel like, It really pays to invest in anything and probably everything especially of note and have a mind set of getting the best out of it all.

This scenario is base on my personal experience and acquaintance with someone and I wonder why it is that way. The person in question is a student, a very intelligent and brilliant one who is ready to be the best in his chosen field. Right from time he always studies his books everyday even before the exam, He had cultivated this habit to the extent that he never left a stone untouched even if not perfectly but he made sure he always take his time to go through them all. And not to be amazed, all his examination results were very good and prove that his effort had really paid off.

But one remarkable thing happen that nearly made him want to give up or sell out. He studied for a particular course so hard that he couldn't sleep for almost a week trying to do what he does best which was reading. On the faithful day of the examination, he was convinced that he was ready for the examination. He did the paper and came out of the hall with a smiling face hoping to have an excellent result in that particular course but to his greatest surprise and amusement he had a 'credit pass', to others they feel this was a good result at least he doesn't have to carry over the course but to him that was a very discouraging result compare to those efforts he had put to it in achieving the best. His friend who had pick up the hand-out a day to the exam also had a credit pass. This was what really discourages him and he said to himself "what a wasted effort" to have read so much and at the end of the day having the same grade as someone who read a day to the examination.

A thought immediately came to his mind to treat future examinations with less effort so as to avoid wasting so much precious time. He decided to adapt to this new principle of his and see what the outcome is going to be like. In his mind, he knew it was a bad idea but the fact remains that his old principle is stronger than he thought. He had been more used to reading and it had become his whole habit to always read even before examination season. Then he started coming back to his right senses as to ignore the bad thought and listen to the good and right one. He concluded by saying success is not to be dictated by exam scores or grades but by how much knowledge he had in him and how to use it to the benefit himself and even the world at large. Then he vow to always pray to God for uncommon favour in any of his endeavor.

The student here is me and I am so glad that I didn't listen to the bad thought that overcame me in my sad moment. I encourage everyone out there to emulate me. There is always a price to pay and the reward of effort is ultimate success which we can always be proud of.

Emotional challenges are also very important and I will say nobody is perfectly capable to handle it because it has to do with the individual inner being. It involves trying to control and to merge different things that are arousing together and still be able to take care of other things without affecting the individual ethical. This is so much challenging and can be build upon or develop or become knowledgeable as the individual grows up and become matured or established.

But my most fearful challenge is the issue of expressing myself to a large number of people who are ready to judge or appreciate me. I have this phobia of public speaking and I never knew until when am seasoned enough to experience such scenario.

This is so much private and confidential to me but never the less; I will still share it for teens to learn and take note of. This scenario started unveiling itself when I had to talk to few people about how I feel about them. I discovered I can blend in with few people like two to three to about ten people maximum and still communicate well but when it got to more than that. I started trembling, my heart beat faster, I started shaking and feeling uncomfortable anymore. Then I realise I had a phobia in that area. I tried so much to fight it but it seems it had gathered so much power than I expected. Then I know definitely that I needed help but where will the helps comes from? It has to come from someone close to me, someone who knows what I am feeling at a particular time and understand me for who I am. Someone that can encourage me to express myself at length and be ready to get my back on my feet in case of any fall or flop. Unfortunately that person was far away from me in distance and to express this via virtual platform is definitely not okay by me. This means I am in trouble because I definitely have to free myself from this phobia, and I need encouragement but was nowhere to be found.

My worse pain about this is that it makes me looks different and being of a low self esteem which I know am not. Am tired of seeing my mate overcoming this phobia an here I am still fighting mine. I know we are all different and there is no point at all for me to compare myself with somebody else but I don't want to be inferior to an abstract phenomenon nevertheless how am I going to prove that. I thought to myself that I have to find another way to speak for myself, another way to show the whole world that I have something to offer and am ready to deliver my part, to fill the void which is the purpose of my existence and to write my name in the wall of time that I was once here and I made my own contribution like everyone else . . . I sense I could put all my thought, feelings and lessons, experiences into writing which I think will even speak and propel me to greater height.

Thinking of all these, I knew I can do it myself I mean be what I want to be without any fear in mind. I learnt a great lesson one day when I went to watch a street football in another area very close to mine, during the cause of the match, something transpire and it nearly led to a street fight which I was afraid of at first but along the line the courage came from nowhere and am ready to blend in and stop my friends from fighting instead of me running away because that was initially what was on my mind. I learnt that day that when you face your worse fear, and you are determined to scale through then **the natural courage will come along and see you through**. This life, we are all afraid of one thing or the other but when we let the fear overwhelms us, we lose sight of victory.

One faithful day, I and a group of friends attended a conference and at night, we were in our hotel room gisting about what transpire the whole day during the sessions and training we had. We were seven in number and one of us made a suggestion to describe each of us in less than three sentences. This was fun I thought in my mind, not knowing the outcome and consequences of such game. The first person started by defining each of us based on his knowledge and the time he had spent with each of us. We all took turns to do the same and to my amusement and biggest surprise, all the comments and definition they attached to me was undeniable and incontrovertible. They were the actual features that existed in me and they all said different things about me based on their individual acquaintance with me. These goes for us all. Some of these comments I was proud of when they mention them and others I was ashamed of but I know that is the real me. With this little game of ours, I will establish the fact that you know yourself more than anybody does and that whether you like it or not people are observing and noticing you in your everyday endeavour and they also have some comment to pass about who you are, and it turns out that most times they are always right and that doesn't give you the right to denied any of it especially when you know that they are correct but it hurts you to admits the raw facts.

This little scenario was a challenge to me because I found out that almost all my friends knows my strength and weaknesses and it might be use against me one day either now or later. Well that was my own thought and this thought gives rise to the fact that I was scared of not ready or will not even be able to improve on those weaknesses and this bad feelings usually gives rise to inferiority complex because the fact had already been established that the other person is better than me in a particular area and this will make me not to even try at all to develop myself as regards that. On the other hand, it gives me the courage to develop and explore my weakness and use them in my favour because it will suddenly amazed my mate that what they know about me as regards that aspect is not accurate again and I might have a strange grips on them all. This feeling usually goes for every average teen.

CONCLUSION

As a teenager, every time I opened my eye to the brightness of the day, to the beautiful blue sky and the marvellous green field, I am always amazed by the perfectness of nature.

I always took time to think of my responsibility in advance. The future is so much fast approaching and I kept asking myself, can I make it, Can I survive the future storm, what if I freak out. Every time I have this thought my instincts tells me to always remember to breath. I am always scared of what lies ahead. My father had done his part by taking care of his responsibility to a particular point and that he deserve to be given an award for a job well done, and very soon he will be passing the baton or wand of responsibility to me. He had survives his own challenges and difficulties and in no time he will be a champion. And as a matter of facts he and everyone else is expecting much more from me, to be more victorious than he was as a result of the advantages that I have and he doesn't. As a teen I know that very soon it will be my turn to start the race of life and to make sure that in every ramification that I run fast ahead of my father, by doing these, he will be proud of me. He has taken his time to train me well purposely for these days to come. He had impacted in me the necessary knowledge to survive the race. Now I am on my own, to prove to my father and the entire human races that I am capable to partake in the race of life and to also run fast above the very expectation set for me.

Right now with all these before me, I have to be prepared, I have to summon all the courage I can possibly get to help me partake in the race and not only that but to also win the race so that my father can be proud enough to say "this is my son" and for the whole world to celebrate my existence.

All these I felt as a teenager, and all these I have recorded in this book to help today's teen and the coming teenagers learn from and to also make them understand that this is the cross road in life. Either you are here or not. But when you are sure that you are indeed here, then your presence had to be announced by the work of your hand. Let us together start from this tender age to raise the flag to a higher ground. The presence of this book in your hand shows that I have done my own part; I am announced by this book and now it is your turn. Discover what your passions are and don't waste time but follow them. The question is will you do your part and if yes, when will that be? Generations are patiently waiting for our manifestation. Now is the time for it to spring forth. I will spare one of my favourite quotes which say **"at a time, there is no time"**

This is the cross road, when you grow old and look back and thinks what if. **We will all be bothered by the things we did not attempt rather than things we did. It up to you . . .**

NOTES

Milton Keynes UK
Ingram Content Group UK Ltd.
UKHW011724250424
441687UK00015B/125